The Jamestown Colony

by Melissa Higgins

Content Consultant
Tim McNeese
Associate Professor of History, York College

CORE
LIBRARY

Published by ABDO Publishing Company, PO Box 398166, Minneapolis, MN 55439. Copyright © 2013 by Abdo Consulting Group, Inc. International copyrights reserved in all countries. No part of this book may be reproduced in any form without written permission from the publisher. The Core Library™ is a trademark and logo of ABDO Publishing Company.

Printed in the United States of America, North Mankato, Minnesota
112012
012013

♻ THIS BOOK CONTAINS AT LEAST 10% RECYCLED MATERIALS.

Editor: Mirella Maxwell
Series Designer: Becky Daum

Cataloging-in-Publication Data
Higgins, Melissa.
 The Jamestown Colony / Melissa Higgins.
  p. cm. -- (Foundations of our nation)
Includes bibliographical references and index.
ISBN 978-1-61783-710-4
1. Jamestown (Va.)--History--17th century--Juvenile literature. 2. Jamestown (Va.)--Colonial period, ca. 1600-1775--Juvenile literature. I. Title.
975.5--dc22

                                                    2012946532

Photo Credits: North Wind/North Wind Picture Archive, cover, 1, 8, 15, 18, 20, 23, 25, 26, 33, 36, 39; Shutterstock Images, 4, 45; Georgios Kollidas/Shutterstock Images, 7; National Geographic/Getty Images, 10; iStockphoto, 12, 30; Bettman/Corbis/AP Images, 28

Cover: Captain John Smith explored the Chesapeake Bay region in the early 1600s.

CONTENTS

CHAPTER ONE

Voyage to Virginia: In Search of Riches

On December 20, 1606, three ships sailed down the Thames River in England. The buildings of central London stood behind them. A months-long journey across the Atlantic Ocean was ahead of the ships. The passengers were both excited and afraid as they imagined lives of leisure and riches in a New World paradise. This was what the Virginia Company had promised them.

Tourists can visit replicas of the Virginia-bound ships, the Susan Constant, Godspeed, and Discovery, in Virginia.

Captain Christopher Newport commanded the flagship, the *Susan Constant*. Together, the three ships carried 39 crew members and 104 passengers. They were men and boys from different backgrounds. But they all shared the goal of becoming the first settlers in a new colony. They were headed to the Chesapeake Bay in a territory called Virginia more than 6,000 miles (9,656 km) away.

Not the First

These colonists would not be the first Europeans to travel to the New World. In the 1500s, Spanish ships explored the Chesapeake Bay. These ships were looking for a trade route to China. English explorers also investigated the area. Both the Spanish and the English left in the late 1500s and returned to Europe.

Englishman Sir Walter Raleigh started a colony near the Chesapeake Bay at Roanoke in 1584.

And Algonquian Native Americans had been living in the Chesapeake Bay long before the first Europeans arrived.

Settlements for Profit

In 1603, the English government stopped allowing merchants to raid foreign ships. Merchants had to look for other sources of income. Colonies were one source. A merchant company would attract men with

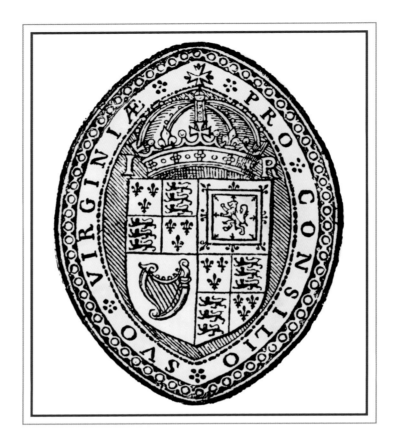

The seal of the Virginia Company.

the promise of adventure and riches. In return, these colonists would mine for precious metals and search for a trade route to China. They would also trade with the Native Americans in exchange for valuable goods. These goods could then be shipped back to England to be sold.

In 1606, the Virginia Company received a charter from King James I. The charter created two separate companies: the Plymouth Company and the London Company. The Plymouth Company planned to start a colony in what would become Maine. The London Company chose the Chesapeake Bay.

A Long Voyage

Because of bad weather, the three ships bound for the Chesapeake Bay were delayed for six weeks along the European coast. The passengers thought about returning home. But the weather finally changed. The ships sailed south along the coast of Europe and then on to North Africa.

The long delay cut into supplies. The ships

The Trade Winds

The trade winds of the Atlantic Ocean flow in a giant circle between Europe, North Africa, and the Americas. When traveling west in the early 1600s, ships sailed at the bottom of the circle, off of North Africa. This was not the quickest route. But it was the most reliable. Within a few years, ships began sailing straight west to save time. Ships took the more direct route east on the return voyage to Europe.

9

The cross marks the spot where colonists first landed. It was named Cape Henry in honor of King James's son.

made several stops along the route to pick up fresh food and water.

On April 26, 1607, the 104 colonists finally reached the Chesapeake Bay. After more than four months at sea, the land was a welcome sight. It looked like paradise.

The colonists hoped the Algonquians would be friendly. But as the landing party returned to the ship, arrows wounded two of the colonists. An Englishman fired back with a musket. It would be the first of many conflicts.

These verses are taken from "To the Virginia Voyage," written in 1606 by Michael Drayton. The poem was written in honor of the proposed new colony. Read the poem carefully. What is the main idea the poet is trying to get across?

> And cheerfully at sea,
> Successe you still entice,
>   To get the pearl and gold,
>   And ours to hold
> Virginia,
> Earth's onely paradise.
>
> Where nature hath in store
> Fowle, Venison, and Fish,
>   And the fruitful'st Soyle
>   Without your toyle,
> Three Harvests more,
> All greater than your wish.

Source: David A Price. *Love and Hate in Jamestown: John Smith, Pocahontas, and the Start of a New Nation. New York: Random House, 2003. Print. 13-15.*

Consider Your Audience

Imagine you want to convince someone to take a voyage to a strange new land. How could you rewrite the poem for a different audience? Try adapting it for your parents, your principal, or your friends.

CHAPTER TWO

A Difficult Beginning

Within 24 hours of sighting land, the colonists opened a sealed box with orders from the Virginia Company. It included the names of the colony's first seven council members. These men would govern the new colony. No one was surprised the list included six English gentlemen. The big surprise was Captain John Smith.

Captain John Smith was a professional soldier hired for his military abilities.

Along the journey, the ship officers had accused Smith of planning mutiny. They placed him under arrest. He was still a prisoner when the fleet reached the New World. Smith disliked that the colony would be led by men with social connections. He thought the colony should be led by men with skills and knowledge—like him.

"James Towne"

The next step was finding a site for the new colony. On May 14, 1607, the colonists anchored their ships in the James River and brought supplies ashore. They named the colony Jamestown (James Towne) in honor of King James I.

John Smith: Adventurer and Writer

John Smith was born in 1580. He left home seeking adventure at age 16. While fighting as a soldier, he was captured and sold as a slave. He escaped and went back to England. Smith was 26 years old when he was asked to join the Jamestown expedition. Smith drew maps of the Chesapeake Bay area, kept journals, and wrote books about his time in Virginia.

The Jamestown settlement was 35 miles (55 km) inland along the James River.

The men began clearing the area of trees and planting gardens. The colonists pitched canvas tents to live in. They put off unloading their guns and building defenses. The colonists wanted to show the Algonquians they were friendly.

Problems in Jamestown

The colonists soon learned why no Native Americans were living on the site they had chosen. It was an unhealthy place to live. The land was marshy and filled with mosquitos. It didn't have fresh water during the summer. By August, men began to sicken and die.

The colonists also didn't have enough food. Much of the food they brought to survive the first winter had already been eaten. Because of their late arrival, the colonists were unable to plant enough crops. A severe drought meant many of the crops they had planted weren't thriving.

Poor leadership and idleness also caused many problems in the new colony. The leaders were

Who Were the Jamestown Colonists?

About 47 of the first Jamestown colonists were gentlemen in their 20s and 30s with business and social connections. There were also 12 skilled craftsmen. The remaining 41 colonists were made up of seamen and laborers. There were also four boys.

FURTHER EVIDENCE

There is quite a bit of information about Captain John Smith in Chapter Two. It also covers the beginnings of the Jamestown Colony. What is the main point of this chapter? What key evidence supports this point? Go to the article on John Smith at the Web site below. Find a quote from the Web site that supports the chapter's main point. Does the quote support an existing piece of evidence in the chapter? Does it add a new one?

Captain John Smith
www.apva.org/rediscovery/page.php?page_id=25

overwhelmed by the hard circumstances. They argued about what to do.

In addition, the Native Americans confused and frightened the colonists. Some attacked. Others were friendly. They spoke a different language. As a result, there were many misunderstandings between the Native Americans and the colonists.

In late May, the settlement was attacked by hundreds of Native Americans. The colonists fired a ship's cannon at the Native Americans before

The painting, *above*, shows colonists defending the colony from attacks by Native Americans.

the colony could be overrun. After the attack, the colonists worked to improve their defenses. By June 14, the colonists had built a triangular palisade with raised watchtowers at each corner.

On June 22, 1607, Captain Newport and his crew sailed for England with the *Susan Constant* and the *Godspeed* to report the colony's progress to the Virginia Company. They left the *Discovery* for the colony to use. The colonists were on their own in the New World.

In his book *The Generall Historie of Virginia, New England & the Summer Isles*, Vol. 1, John Smith wrote about 1607 Jamestown. Some of his accounts described the food they had to eat in order to survive:

> [W]hilest the ships stayed, our allowance was somewhat bettered, by a daily proportion of Bisket. . . . But when they departed, there remained neither taverne, beere house, nor place of reliefe, but the common Kettell . . . and that was halfe a pint of wheat, and as much barley boyled with water for a man a day, and this . . . contained as many wormes as grains.
>
> . . .
>
> At this time our diet was for most part water and bran, and three ounces of little better stuffe in bread for five men a meale, and thus we lived neere three months.

> Source: John Smith. The Generall Historie of Virginia, New England & the Summer Isles, Vol I. New York: Macmillan Company. 1907. Print. 318-319.

Nice View

After reading this passage, review the poem at the end of Chapter 1. Write a short essay comparing the two works. What is the point of view of each author? If there are similarities, what are they? How are they different, and why?

CHAPTER THREE

John Smith Takes Charge

By September 1607, approximately half of the Jamestown colonists had died. Smith used his experience as a soldier to help the remaining colonists survive. He led explorations and learned the differences between the Native American leaders and tribes.

Smith began to learn Algonquian languages. This helped him barter for food with the Native Americans.

The Great Powhatan

The Algonquians weren't the only Native Americans in the area. The Chesapeake Bay area was part of a growing Native American empire in the early 1600s. Its leader was a powerful chief named Powhatan.

In December 1607, Powhatan's brother, Opechancanough, captured Smith while he was exploring. Smith was brought before Powhatan and placed on the ground. Club-wielding warriors surrounded Smith.

Suddenly, Powhatan's 11-year-old daughter Pocahontas rushed to Smith's side. She held her head over his. Scholars believe she was playing a role in an adoption ceremony. Powhatan's strategy was to gain

Chief Powhatan was estimated to be in his 60s or 70s when the colonists arrived. He was described as a majestic figure who inspired awe in those who met him.

control over the English colony by including one of its leaders in Powhatan society. Powhatan gave Smith land to govern and made him one of his chiefs.

New Arrivals

By January 1608, only 38 of the original 104 colonists were still alive. Virginia had not been the paradise the colonists had expected. The council of leaders decided to abandon the colony and return to England. But just days after this decision, Captain Newport arrived with food, supplies, and approximately 60 new colonists. For the moment, the original colonists decided to stay put.

John Smith: President of Jamestown

Later that spring, Smith set out to explore and map the Chesapeake Bay region. While Smith was out exploring, the new arrivals also began getting sick.

The colonists were running out of food again. And yet they were doing little work to prepare for winter.

When Smith returned to the colony, he was one of the last able-bodied council members. He became council president on September 10, 1608.

Searching for Gold

Captain Newport was determined to find gold near Jamestown. He ordered the colonists to spend hours digging in the mud for gold. Newport and the colonists were never successful. The closest they came to finding gold turned out to be fool's gold.

Some believe Pocahontas risked her life to save Smith.
Others believe it was part of an adoption ceremony.

He immediately put the colonists to work. They harvested the struggling crops and practiced their shooting skills. The colony was finally on a course toward stability and survival.

After Smith put the colonists to work, they built a storehouse, a church, and several houses within the palisade.

Two Demands

Captain Newport arrived again in late September 1608 with 70 more colonists, including the colony's first women. He also brought two demands from the Virginia Company. First: the colonists needed to find something of value. Second: the colonists needed to put a crown on Powhatan's head. This would place him under the control of King James I. They hoped Powhatan would be honored and supply Jamestown with food and goodwill.

The plan backfired. Angered, Powhatan no longer allowed his people to bargain with the colonists for food. He was going to starve the English out.

EXPLORE ONLINE

This chapter had a lot of information about the relationship between the Jamestown colonists and the Native Americans in the area. You can find even more information about this relationship at the Web site below. Compare and contrast the information on the Web site with the information in this book. What can you learn from the Web site about what items were popular to trade, why they were traded, and how they were made?

Trade

www.apva.org/rediscovery/page.php?page_id=70

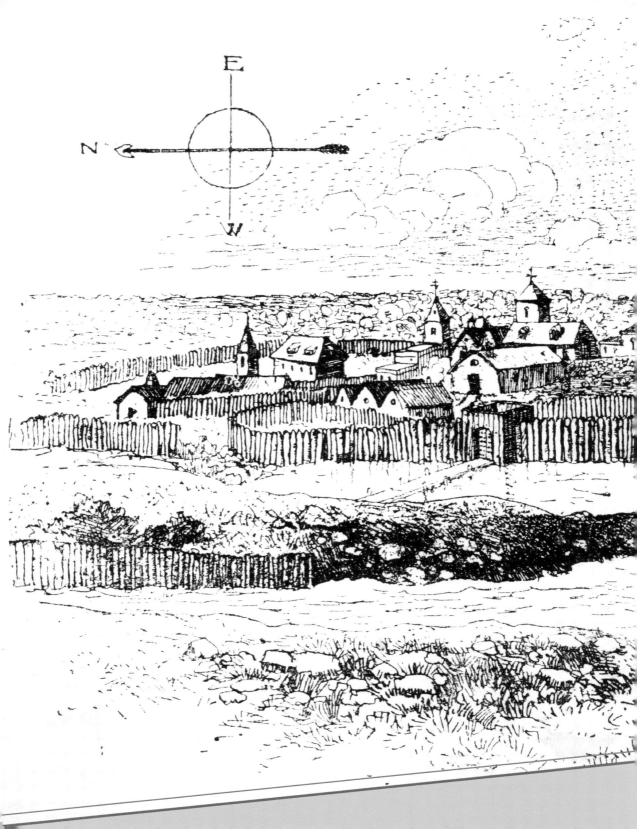

CHAPTER FOUR

Struggle for Survival

Newport's ship left Jamestown in December 1608. He left 200 colonists behind to face another harsh winter and decreasing food supplies. There were not enough trained hunters or fishermen to feed everyone. Smith began threatening the village chiefs. Some chiefs agreed to share their food with the colonists despite Powhatan's orders.

The Jamestown Colony was not ready to face another harsh winter.

With Smith's new rule in place, the men built 20 more houses. They also built a sturdier fort.

But it was a cold winter. Some villages had no grain to spare.

Smith bartered enough to allow the colony to survive until the next harvest. But while Smith was away getting food, the colonists did little work. He made a new rule: *He that will not work shall not eat.*

Smith's rule put the colonists to work. He separated the colony into small groups to save grain. These groups were sent away from Jamestown where they could live off whatever other food they could gather or hunt.

More Colonists

On August 11, 1609, four ships arrived at Jamestown.

By now, the colony had been in existence for more than two years. There were now about 500 colonists. And most of them had just arrived. Many of the newcomers focused on finding riches. Conflict continued between the new settlers and different tribes.

Pocahontas: Friend to Jamestown

Pocahontas was born around 1595. She served as a trader to Jamestown and a frequent messenger for her father. She also became a good friend of Smith. In 1613, Pocahontas met John Rolfe, a tobacco planter. She converted to Christianity and married Rolfe on April 5, 1614. Pocahontas died in England in March 1617, at age 22.

During one peace-making trip, Smith's gunpowder bag accidentally caught fire and seriously burned his leg. Due to his injury, Smith returned to England in September 1609.

The Starving Time

After Smith left, John Percy was elected president. Powhatan took the opportunity to wage war on the scattered settlements. He again hoped to starve the English out. Many settlers returned to the safety of the Jamestown Fort. Food supplies soon began shrinking as colonists stopped hunting and gathering and stayed at the fort. Powhatan had boats cut from the English docks. He ordered all of the fort's hogs slaughtered.

The winter of 1609 to 1610 would become known as "The Starving Time."

And his warriors killed colonists who wandered out to find food.

Starving colonists at the fort ate their horses, cats, and dogs. Then they ate rats and mice. They even ate the leather from their shoes. By March 1610, less than 100 Jamestown colonists remained.

A Message

On May 24, 1610, Sir Thomas Gates, the new governor, and the rest of his party landed at Jamestown. Nine months earlier, a hurricane had blown their wrecked ship to Bermuda. Gates was so shocked by the conditions of Jamestown that he decided to bring everyone back to England. The miserable colonists happily agreed.

But a boatman met the colonists as they were leaving the Chesapeake Bay. Three ships were coming. They carried 150 new settlers and plenty of supplies. Gates and his passengers reluctantly returned to Jamestown.

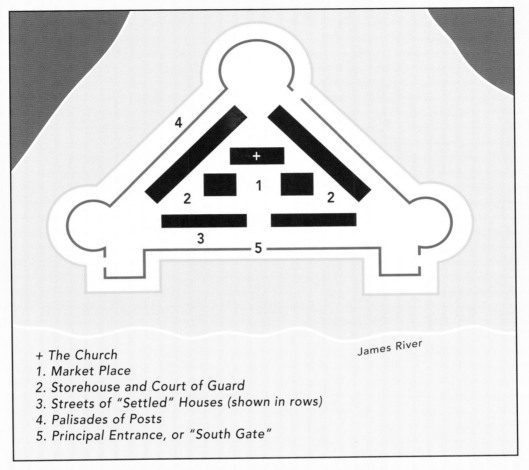

+ The Church
1. Market Place
2. Storehouse and Court of Guard
3. Streets of "Settled" Houses (shown in rows)
4. Palisades of Posts
5. Principal Entrance, or "South Gate"

James River

Jamestown Fort

Study this overhead drawing of the Jamestown Fort in 1608. How does the information presented compare to what you have learned from the text about the palisade and the buildings within it? How are the images similar to what you have learned? How are they different?

The newest supply fleet arrived 19 days later and contained enough food to last the colony a year. "The Starving Time" was over.

CHAPTER FIVE

A Successful Settlement

Sir Thomas Dale became governor in 1612. He thought the colonists were lazy and made tough new rules. People who got to work late or quit early were whipped. Those who ran away to join the Powhatans might be hanged, burned, or tortured. Death was a common punishment.

A colonial map of Virginia

Tobacco

The colonists finally had enough to eat. This meant they were able to focus on finding ways to make money. Tobacco had been popular in Europe since Spanish explorers brought it back from the Caribbean around 1500. John Rolfe, Pocahontas's husband, had tobacco seeds shipped from Trinidad and Venezuela. Then he planted the tobacco in Jamestown. Other colonists followed Rolfe's lead. Virginia tobacco became a hit in England. In August 1620, the colony exported 50,000 pounds (23,000 kg) of leaves.

The Beginnings of a New Nation

In 1619, the Virginia Company decided to give land to the colonists. This made colonists more excited about

Jamestown finally had a moneymaking export. Tobacco sales helped the colony thrive and grow.

building a house, planting crops, and raising families. Now, America, not England, was their home.

The Virginia Company also began a new form of government in Jamestown. This new local government, called the General Assembly, had its first meeting on July 30, 1619. The General Assembly had to remain loyal to England. But it could make decisions and pass laws. This was the first representative government in an English colony in America.

A Model Colony

In 1624, the Virginia Company lost its charter. Virginia became a royal colony. Jamestown had a profitable trade tobacco. It had a representative government. Its citizens owned land. The colony was a success.

More Conflicts

After Powhatan died, his brother Opechancanough took control of the empire. He was angry with the English and attacked on March 22, 1622. His warriors killed nearly 350 of the 1,200 colonists. But Opechancanough would never defeat the English. Eventually, most of the Powhatans moved away. Others became part of the colony.

The Jamestown Colony had experienced many hard times. Between 1607 and 1624, three-fourths of the 6,000 colonists died. Jamestown also represented the beginning of the end for many Native American tribes and their way of life.

Jamestown had many successes too. It was the first model English colony. It was also the beginning of

Population of Jamestown Over Time

The population of Jamestown varied greatly until it finally reached steady growth in 1622. How does the information presented in this chart compare to what you have read in the text about the events affecting the colony's population? How are they similar? How are they different?

Date	Population	Reason for Change
May 1607	104	First arrivals
December 1607	38	Starvation
October 1608	200	New arrivals
Summer 1609	131	Death from diseases
August 1609	381	New arrivals
October 1609	280	Native American attacks
May 1610	90	"The Starving Time"
June 1610	375	New arrivals
December 1610	250	Disease; Native American attacks
Late March 1611	152	Departures; Native American attacks
Late May 1611	482	New arrivals
August 1611	752	New arrivals
December 1611	600	Native American attacks
1615	400	New arrivals
1622	1,240	New arrivals
1625	1,300	New arrivals

a new country. The foundations of the United States were firmly in place.

IMPORTANT DATES

1606

On December 20, the ships Susan Constant, Godspeed, and Discovery leave from London, England, for Virginia.

1607

On April 26, 104 English colonists reach Virginia. They establish Jamestown on May 14.

1608

In the spring, a supply ship arrives carrying approximately 60 new colonists.

1612

Sir Thomas Dale, Jamestown's new governor, imposes new laws.

1613

The Jamestown Colony continues to harvest tobacco.

1614

Pocahontas marries John Rolfe on April 5.

1608

Captain John Smith becomes the Jamestown council president on September 10.

1609

On August 11, four supply ships arrive with new colonists.

1610

Sir Thomas Gates arrives on May 24 after being stuck in Bermuda.

1619

The General Assembly has its first meeting on July 30.

1622

On March 22, forces led by Powhatan's brother, Opechancanough, attack, killing nearly as many as 350 colonists.

1624

The Virginia Company loses its charter, and Virginia becomes a royal colony.

Why Do I Care?

Come up with two or three ways the Jamestown Colony connects to your life. For example, how would your life be different if a country other than England, such as Spain, had first settled most of America? Imagine what your life would be like if America had a king or a queen instead of a democracy.

Another View

Find another source about the Jamestown Colony (or one of the subjects covered in this book). Write a short essay comparing and contrasting its point of view with that of this book's author. Be sure to answer these questions: What is the point of view of each author? How are they similar and why? How are they different and why?

Surprise Me

Think about what you learned from this book. List the two or three facts in this book that you found most surprising. Write a short paragraph about each, describing what you found surprising and why.

You Are There

Imagine you are living in the same village as Pocahontas during 1607. Write 300 words describing your life. What do you see happening in your village? What do you eat? What are your siblings doing? What is it like seeing Englishmen for the first time?

GLOSSARY

Algonquian
Native Americans who share the Algonquian languages

barter
trade for goods and services

charter
a written grant from a government

colony
an area of land under control of another country

drought
an unusually long period of little or no rainfall

flagship
the ship in a fleet that carries the commanding officer

fool's gold
a yellow-colored mineral resembling gold

musket
a rifle with a long barrel loaded from the muzzle

mutiny
open rebellion against authority

palisade
a wall of upright logs

LEARN MORE

Books

Harkins, William H. and Susan Sales Harkins. *Jamestown: The First Colony*. Hockessin, DE: Mitchell Lane Publishers, 2006.

Pederson, Charles E. *The Jamestown Colony*. Edina, MN: ABDO Publishing Company, 2009.

Petrie, Kristin. *John Smith*. Edina, MN: ABDO Publishing Company, 2007.

Web Links

To learn more about the Jamestown Colony, visit ABDO Publishing Company online at **www.abdopublishing.com**. Web sites about Jamestown are featured on our Book Links page. These links are routinely monitored and updated to provide the most current information available. Visit **www.mycorelibrary.com** for free additional tools for teachers and students.

INDEX

ABOUT THE AUTHOR

Melissa Higgins is the author of many nonfiction books for children and young adults. She also writes short stories and novels. Before pursuing a writing career, Ms. Higgins worked as a counselor in schools and private practice.